CINCO DE MAYO

LESLIE C. KAPLAN

The Library of
HOLIDAYS™

The Rosen Publishing Group's
PowerKids Press™
New York

To Dad

Published in 2004 by The Rosen Publishing Group, Inc.
29 East 21st Street, New York, NY 10010

First Edition

Editor: Jannell Khu

Book Design: Michael J. Caroleo and Michael de Guzman

Layout: Nick Sciacca

Photo Credits: Cover, p. 15 © Richard Cummins/CORBIS; p. 4 © Morton Beebe/CORBIS; p. 7 © CORBIS; p. 8 © Charles & Josette Lenars/CORBIS; pp. 11, 12 © Bettmann/CORBIS; p. 16 © Jan Butchofsky-Houser/CORBIS; p. 19 © Robert Holmes/CORBIS; p. 20 © IndexStock; p. 22 © Joseph Sohm; ChromoSohm Inc./CORBIS.

Kaplan, Leslie C.
   Cinco de Mayo / Leslie C. Kaplan.
      p. cm. — (The library of holidays)
   Includes bibliographical references and index.
   ISBN 0-8239-6662-3 (library binding)
   1. Cinco de Mayo (Mexican holiday)—Juvenile literature.   2. Cinco de Mayo, Battle of, 1862—Juvenile literature.   3. Mexico—Social life and customs—Juvenile literature.   4. Juárez, Benito, 1806–1872—Juvenile literature.   I. Title.   II. Series.
   F1233.K27 2003
   394.26972—dc21

2002009478

Manufactured in the United States of America

CONTENTS

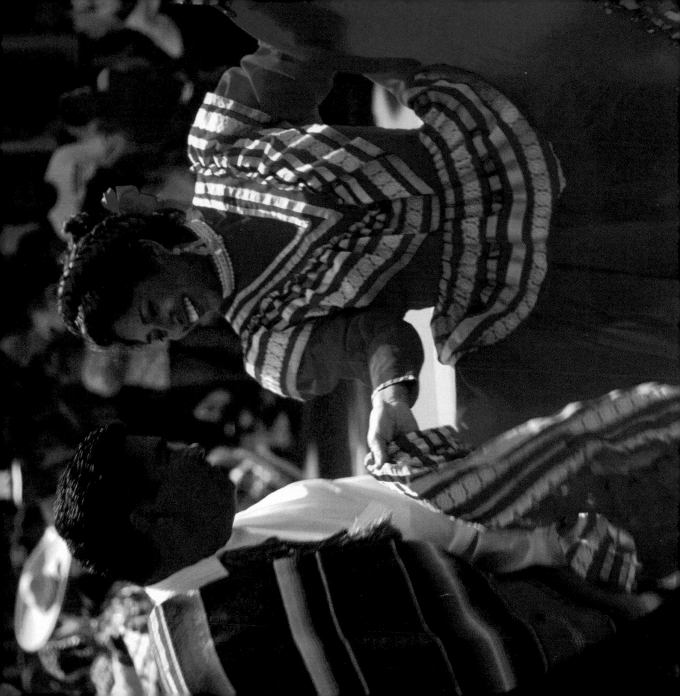

WHAT IS CINCO DE MAYO?

Cinco de Mayo is Spanish for "fifth of May." On this holiday, Mexicans remember the famous battle that was fought in Puebla, Mexico, on May 5, 1862. They are proud of their Mexican **ancestors**, who **defeated** the French in that battle. Cinco de Mayo fiestas are held in Mexico and in the United States where many Mexicans and Mexican Americans live. Fiestas are celebrations, or parties. On May 5, many people show their love for Mexico by wearing the red, white, and green colors of the Mexican flag.

▲ Cinco de Mayo fiestas can include dancing, parades, and speeches. These dancers are wearing Mexican costumes.

TROUBLE IN MEXICO

During the mid-nineteenth century, Mexico fought several wars to keep its independence. Wars are expensive. Mexico had to borrow money from other countries, including France. In 1861, Mexican president Benito Juárez announced that Mexico could not pay back the borrowed money for two years. He wanted to use the money that was left in the **treasury** to help his own people. This angered French **emperor** Napoléon III. In 1861, he sent an army to attack Mexico. He wanted Mexico to be a part of the French **Empire**.

French emperor Charles-Louis-Napoléon Bonaparte believed that his powerful French army could easily defeat Mexico. ▲

THE BATTLE OF PUEBLA

Mexican general Ignacio Zaragoza did not expect his small, poorly trained army to win the Battle of Puebla. He hoped to delay the French long enough for the soldiers in Mexico City to prepare to fight. On May 5, 1862, French soldiers stormed up the hills of Puebla. The Mexicans did not have enough guns and **shells** for a long battle. Then it rained and the hills became too slippery for the French to climb. Three times they charged, and each time the Mexicans fought them off. Finally, the French gave up. The Mexicans won!

▲ *Titled The Triumph of Juárez, this painting shows France's defeat at the Battle of Puebla. President Juárez is shown in the top right corner.*

9

A NEW HOLIDAY

A year after the Battle of Puebla, France took control of Mexico. However, the success at Puebla gave Mexico the spirit to fight back. Mexico defeated France in April 1867, and Juárez became president again. To honor the soldiers who won against the French soldiers, he made Cinco de Mayo a national holiday.

Cinco de Mayo and Mexican Independence Day are the two biggest historic celebrations in Mexico. September 16, 1821, is recognized as Mexican Independence Day. This holiday celebrates Mexico's freedom from Spain.

This drawing shows a Mexican Independence Day parade that took place in the 1800s.

People honor Benito Juárez on Cinco de Mayo. Juárez is considered Mexico's greatest president. Juárez was born to a poor Mexican family. His parents died when he was three years old. He was then raised by his uncle, who taught him to read. At age 25, Juárez became a **lawyer**. He often helped poor people who could not pay him for his services. Later Juárez worked for the government. In 1861, he became Mexico's president. Juárez's strong leadership helped Mexico to defeat France.

▲ Benito Juárez is called the Mexican Abraham Lincoln for his ability to hold a nation together during a war.

RELIVING THE BATTLE OF PUEBLA

The high point of many Cinco de Mayo celebrations is a **reenactment** of the Battle of Puebla. Some of these pretend battles can last all day! The actors who play French soldiers dress in red and blue uniforms, as the French troops did in 1862. The men who play Mexican soldiers wear straw hats and old, worn clothing. The men carry fake guns, and some soldiers ride horses. The reenactment is a special way to remember the heroes who fought bravely for Mexico's independence.

On May 5, reenactments bring the Battle of Puebla to life throughout Mexico and in some cities in the United States. ▲

Listening to mariachi music is another important Cinco de Mayo **tradition**. Mariachi bands play Mexican **folk songs** on instruments such as the violin and the guitar. The band members are called mariachis. Mariachi bands can have from three to twelve or more members. Their folk songs tell stories of love, death, and war. People sing along and clap to the songs of mariachi bands at fiestas. The band members wear fancy black suits, colorful shirts, and wide-rimmed hats called sombreros.

▲ *It is almost as much fun to look at the fancy costumes of the mariachis as it is to listen to their music.*

CINCO DE MAYO FEAST

Celebrating Cinco de Mayo with a Mexican feast is a big part of the holiday. Delicious smells fill the air in parks, picnic grounds, and street fairs as family and friends gather to enjoy favorite Mexican foods. Many of the dishes that they may eat are made with corn. Corn is the most important Mexican food **staple**. Corn tortillas are the basis of many Mexican dishes. Tortillas are thin, pancakelike pieces of bread made from ground cornmeal. Eating Mexican food is a wonderful way to celebrate Cinco de Mayo.

A woman prepares corn tortillas. Enchiladas, burritos, fajitas, and quesadillas are often made with corn tortillas. ▲

Children play with piñatas during many Mexican celebrations, including Cinco de Mayo. A piñata is a **container** made from clay or cardboard. It is filled with candies, small toys, and money. Piñatas are covered with **papier-mâché** and decorated with colorful ribbons. For the game, the piñata is tied to a rope and hung from a ceiling or a tree. Blindfolded children take turns hitting the piñata with a stick. When someone finally breaks open a piñata, all the children rush to gather the fallen treats!

▲ *Piñatas are made in different shapes and sizes. Popular piñata shapes are fruits, stars, baskets, and animals.*

There are many ways to celebrate Cinco de Mayo. You and your friends can stage a reenactment of the Battle of Puebla. You can go to Cinco de Mayo fiestas that are held at street fairs and parks. At these events, you can enjoy picnics, puppet shows, and baseball and soccer games. However you celebrate Cinco de Mayo, remember that it is an important holiday for Mexicans and Mexican Americans. Their ancestors won a difficult battle on May 5, 1862. Cinco de Mayo is a holiday that became a **symbol** of Mexican independence.

ancestors (AN-ses-terz) Relatives who lived long ago.

container (kun-TAY-ner) A box that holds things.

defeated (dih-FEET-ed) To have won against someone in a battle.

emperor (EM-per-er) The ruler of an empire, or several countries.

empire (EM-pyr) A large area under one ruler.

folk songs (FOHK SONGZ) Traditional songs of a region or country.

lawyer (LOY-er) A person who gives advice about the law and who speaks for people in court.

papier-mâché (pay-per-mah-SHAY) Paper mixed with water to make a paste that can be molded when wet. When it dries, it becomes hard.

reenactment (ree-uh-NAK-ment) Something that is relived.

shells (SHELZ) Metal holders filled with gun powder. Shells may be fired out of a rifle, a gun, or a cannon.

staple (STAY-pul) A very important and basic food item.

symbol (SIM-bul) An object or a design that stands for something else.

tradition (truh-DIH-shun) A way of doing something that is passed down.

treasury (TREH-zher-ee) A place in which a government's money is kept.

INDEX

B
Battle of Puebla,
9–10, 14, 22

C
corn, 18

F
feast, 18
fiestas, 5, 22
folk songs, 17
France, 6, 10

J
Juárez, Benito, 6,
10, 13

M
mariachi bands,
17
mariachis, 17
Mexican
Independence
Day, 10
Mexico, 5–6, 10,
13–14

N
Napoléon III,
emperor of
France, 6

P
piñatas, 21

R
reenactment, 14,
22

S
Spain, 10

Z
Zaragoza,
Ignacio, 9

WEB SITES

Due to the changing nature of Internet links, PowerKids Press has developed an online list of Web sites related to the subject of this book. This site is updated regularly. Please use this link to access the list:
www.powerkidslinks.com/lhol/cincomay/